Salvation's Sign and Seal

The case for infant baptism

Rodger M. Crooks

D0313697

Christian Focus

© Rodger M. Crooks
ISBN 185792 316 2

Published in 1997
by Christian Focus Publications,
Geanies House, Fearn,
Ross-shire, IV20 1TW, Great Britain.

Cover design by Donna Macleod

CONTENTS

FOREWORD 7

PREFACE 9

1. THE BASIS OF BAPTISM 13

2. THE MEANING OF BAPTISM 27

3. THE SUBJECTS OF BAPTISM 41

4. THE MODE OF BAPTISM 57

5. OTHER ISSUES CONNECTED
WITH BAPTISM 79

AN ANNOTATED BIBLIOGRAPHY 92

DEDICATION
To Joan
for all her love and encouragement

FOREWORD

Martin Luther, the great evangelical reformer, used to say 'I am a baptised man' to remind himself of his spiritual privileges in times of weakness and need.

We modern Christians say that all too rarely, often because we have lost sight of what baptism means, seeing instead only problems and disagreements about it.

Here Dr Rodger Crooks can help us. He faces the problem questions in a biblical, pastoral and reliable way, but, more than that, he reminds us also of the blessings to which baptism points us. I hope *Salvation's Sign and Seal* will help many to discover, or perhaps rediscover, the ways in which baptism is an aid to daily Christian living.

Sinclair B Ferguson
Westminster Theological Seminary
Philadelphia, Pennsylvania

PREFACE

'I want to find out more about infant baptism,' a lady said to me on the way out of church one Sunday morning. 'Could you recommend a book to read?' I have to confess that I was hard pushed to answer her question. Do not get me wrong. It is not that there are no good books on infant baptism available. There are. It is just, in my opinion, that they either focus on a particular aspect of infant baptism and do not cover all the issues, or they are too technical and difficult for the ordinary Christian. Over lunch the next day, I told one of my friends about the lady's request and my dilemma. 'Why don't you write one yourself?' he said. So I did, and this is it!

In this book, I have tried to write for the ordinary Christian. Although there has to be some technical language, I have tried to keep it to a minimum. I have attempted to cover all the major issues – the why, what, who and how of infant baptism – in a plain and simple way. If anyone wants to dig deeper, I have included an annotated bibliography at the end of the book, containing other books that develop the various aspects of infant baptism more fully.

My prayer is that this book will help ordinary Christian people realise that the baptism of believers' children is not, as we have been misled to believe by baptist writers, either a left-over from Roman Catholicism that the Reformers did not weed out of the church, or something based on tradition with no basis in the Bible. My prayer is that ordinary Christians will grasp that the case for infant baptism is strong and convincing, with sturdy roots that go deep down into the Bible's teaching.

Without the help and influence of many people, this book would have been written. It would be extremely wrong of me not to acknowledge my debt to them. My thanks go to:

- The people at Christian Focus Publications, and especially to Malcolm Maclean. Without your trust and guidance, this book would never have seen the light of day.

- The people at Westminster Theological Seminary in Philadelphia, and especially to George Fuller, Al Harris, Harvie Conn and Carol Ajamian. This book was part of my Doctor of Ministry project for Westminster. Without the help and encouragement of these four people, I would never have got it finished.

- Mark and Jane Cain. As Baptists, Mark and Jane will not agree with me. However, the support and love I have received from them, and their congregation in Berwick, Pennsylvania, is a visual-aid of the truth that Christian fellowship is based on the fact that we belong to Jesus, and not because we think the same way about baptism.

- Harry Uprichard. He first introduced me to the idea of the covenant of grace, and patiently sorted out my thinking and answered my questions about infant baptism.

- 1st Dromore, and especially the folk who attend the Evening Service. This book is based on a series of long sermons about baptism that they listened to patiently. It was their positive feedback to these sermons that first put the thought in my mind to get them published.

- My parents, Mervyn and Florence Crooks, and my in-laws, David and Sara Hamilton.

- My children – Rosemary, Martyn and Elizabeth.

- Joan. Her love and encouragement throughout our time in Dromore and during the writing of this book has kept me going when I have often wanted to give up.

- Our great covenant-making and covenant-keeping God, who set his love upon me before time began, sent his Son to die for me, sealed his love to me in my baptism, and called me by his Spirit, not only to faith in his Son, but to be a preacher of the glorious gospel of salvation in Jesus alone by grace alone through faith alone.

1

THE BASIS OF BAPTISM

From a distance, the bungalow looked quite impressive. However, no-one would ever live in it, because there was a huge crack running the height of the gable wall. The reason for this huge crack stemmed from a serious defect in the bungalow's foundations. The builder had not taken enough care with them, and this made the building unsafe. Solid foundations are important in the building trade. They are also important when it comes to baptism.

In my experience as a minister, I have found that the problems people have in understanding baptism can be traced back, almost without exception, to a defective grasp of the foundation upon which the biblical view of baptism rests. This is why we need to think about the basis of baptism before we can look at all the other issues connected with baptism.

What is the basis upon which the ordinance of baptism rests? It is rooted in God's covenant grace. This idea is so crucial that, if we do not understand it, it is likely that we will arrive at unsafe views about the other issues connected with baptism.

But what is God's 'covenant of grace'?

The covenant of grace is the unifying theme of the Bible.

The Bible is not really a single book, but a library of sixty-six different books. Yet the amazing thing about the Bible (and this is one of the indicators that it comes from God) is its unity. There is one theme that runs throughout the length and breadth of the Bible: the covenant of grace.

The word 'covenant' appears 271 times in the Bible, all the way from Genesis 6:18 to Revelation 11:19. When God entered into covenant with his people through Moses, he revealed himself by his covenant name *Yahweh*, the LORD (usually set in capital letters in Bible versions). This is the most common description of God in the Old Testament, occurring some 5,655 times. What we might call the catch-phrase of the covenant of grace is the expression 'I will be their God' or 'I will be your God'. It is found in all the different parts of the Bible, first in Genesis 17:8 and finally in Revelation 21:3 in John's vision of what heaven will be like. The terms 'your God' and 'our God' are also covenantal terms, and they occur 685 times in the Bible, beginning with Genesis 17:7 and ending with Revelation 19:5.

I do not want to overwhelm you with statistics, but you can see that this idea of the covenant of grace runs throughout the Bible, from Genesis to Revelation. So when we base our understanding of baptism on the idea of the covenant of grace, we are not resting Christian doctrine upon a few obscure and isolated texts – as is sometimes suggested. We are basing our views upon the central unifying theme of the Bible.

The covenant of grace is to do with salvation.
This is clear from the very words used: 'covenant' and 'grace'. A covenant implies a commitment. Some people sign what is called 'A Deed of Covenant'. If

they pay United Kingdom Income Tax and pay a certain amount of money themselves for a certain length of time, there is a commitment by the Inland Revenue which provides a refund on the tax they paid on that amount of money.

The word 'grace' reminds us that God's commitment to us is not merited by us. So the term 'the covenant of grace' refers to the commitment God has made in order to save men and women, and to bring them into a right relationship with himself. God promised to do this throughout the Old Testament. He fulfilled that promise in Jesus Christ.

The covenant of grace was necessary because of our sinful status before God.

The Bible makes it clear that the covenant of grace was absolutely necessary because, as the Westminster Confession of Faith puts it, 'the distance between God and his creation is so great'.[1] God had to act in salvation because of our sinful status before him.

How did this sinful status come about? To answer this question, we have to travel back in time to the start of history, to Adam. In the Garden of Eden, God made a commitment to Adam, which is known as 'the covenant of works'. In this covenant, God promised Adam life, if he obeyed God:

> The LORD God commanded the man, 'You are free to eat from any tree in the garden; but you must not eat from the Tree of the Knowledge of Good and Evil, for when you eat of it you will surely die' (Genesis 2:16-17).

Disobedience would bring death, but obedience to this one command would bring life and blessings out of all proportion to the little that was required of Adam. Tragically Adam went his own way and disobeyed God, and Genesis 3:1-13 records the sad story of what is known as 'the Fall'. The Bible makes it clear that Adam was not simply acting on his own behalf. He was acting as a representative for all mankind:

> Sin entered the world through one man [Adam], and death through sin, and in this way death came to all men, because all sinned. ... The result of one trespass [Adam's disobedience] was condemnation for all men (Romans 5:12, 18).

We are familiar with this idea of a representative. For example, in politics, we elect a Member of Parliament to represent us in the House of Commons. We are not personally at Westminster to vote. However, our MP who represents us, votes. Everybody shares in the consequences of our representatives' votes. If they vote for good laws, then we enjoy prosperity. But if they vote for bad laws, then we experience hardship. Adam was our representative. God made the covenant of works, not just with Adam personally, but through him with all mankind. So when Adam, our representative, sinned, we all sinned in him.

The Bible's teaching is summarised in *The Shorter Catechism*: 'Since the covenant was made not only for Adam but also for his natural descendants, all mankind sinned in him and fell with him in his first disobedience.'[2] We are all in this sinful status before God, not simply because we sin individually, but primarily because Adam our representative sinned and we all sinned in him.

What are the consequences of being in this sinful status before God? God warned Adam that, if he sinned, he would die, and that is exactly what happened. If Adam our representative experienced death, then so do we, the people he represented.

The death we experience has several aspects to it. We experience *spiritual death*: this involves separation and alienation from God. We experience *physical death*. Physical death, the separation of the body from the soul, is the direct result of the Fall.

We also experience *social death*, for sin divides us from each other. Genesis 3 records how man was divided from God, and then, in Genesis 4, we come across the story of the first murder when Cain killed Abel. Sin not only alienates us from God, it also alienates us from each other.

Finally we experience *eternal death*, the everlasting separation of the body and soul from God in hell. The catastrophic consequences of Adam's sin for us are summed up in *The Shorter Catechism*:

> By the Fall, all mankind lost fellowship with God
> and brought his anger and curse upon themselves.
> They are therefore subject to all the miseries of this
> life, to death itself, and to the pains of hell forever.[3]

In order to save us from the terrible consequences of our sin, both for this life and the next, God had to act in salvation. This is when God's covenant of grace comes in. It lies in our sinful status before God. Our need of salvation because of our sin is written all over the pages of the Bible.

God took the initiative to save us.

It was God who made the first move to set in motion the great covenant arrangements to save us. Over and over the Bible stresses that we do not come looking for God. Not only are we unable to do so, we are also unwilling to do so. Instead God came looking for us.

Why did God set in motion the covenant of grace? Was it because we deserved his salvation because of who we are or because of what we have done? No! God acted out of sheer grace. He did what he did because he freely and willingly chose to. This is made clear in those wonderful words found in Deuteronomy 7:7-8:

> The LORD did not set his affection on you and choose you because you were more numerous than other people, for you were the fewest of all people. But it was because the LORD loved you ... that he ... redeemed you.

We need to be absolutely clear about this. There is nothing which we have done or can ever hope to do which will make God save us. We have no lever on God. The only reason why God saved us was because of his sovereign grace. He was moved by pity and mercy towards us.

God's purpose in the covenant of grace was to save his people.

The first indication of the covenant of grace is in Genesis 3:15. As part of his judgment on Satan, God said, 'And I will put enmity between you and the woman, and between your offspring and hers; he will crush your head, and you will strike his heel.' This statement contains the covenant of grace in embryo. Its implications are developed in the rest of the Bible. God gives notice that he is going to take the initiative. He says 'I will'. He is promising to save his people through a redeemer: 'I will put enmity between you [Satan] and the woman, and between your offspring and hers; he [Jesus] will crush your head.' The allusion to the woman's offspring, or seed, is a reference to Jesus.

What a gracious God he is! Think about it. Adam and Eve have just recently fallen. They are still hot in their sin. What is God doing? Writing them off? Wiping them off the face of the earth for their rebellion and sin? No! He is offering to save them. What love! What grace!

What would this salvation promised in the covenant of grace be like? The salvation promises are summed up in the catch-phrase of the covenant of grace: 'I will be your God.' That is an umbrella term that covers all God's covenant promises. God promises that when he saves us he will forgive us and cleanse us from our sins; he will make us his friends; he will put his Holy Spirit within us; he will give us the willingness and the ability to keep his law; he will be with us always; and he will take us to be with him in heaven when we die. All those marvellous promises of salvation are included in the covenantal catch-phrase 'I will be your God'. When we come across that expression, we are to read all those promises into it.

Is not the salvation God promises to us in the covenant of grace wonderful and so gracious? We get a flavour of it in the following passages:

This is the covenant I will make with the house of
Israel after that time. I will put my law in their
minds and write it on their hearts. [Here comes the
covenantal catch-phrase.] I will be their God and
they will be my people. No longer will a man teach
his neighbour or a man his brother, saying, 'Know
the LORD' [God's special covenant name], because
they will all know me, from the least of them to the
greatest. For I will forgive their wickedness and will
remember their sins no more (Jeremiah 31:33-34).

I will cleanse you from all your impurities. I will
give you a new heart and put a new spirit in you. I
will remove from you your heart of stone and give
you a heart of flesh. And I will put my Spirit in you
and move you to follow my decrees and be careful
to keep my laws (Ezekiel 36:25-27).

Then I saw a new heaven and a new earth, for the
first heaven and the first earth had passed away, and
there was no longer any sea. I saw the Holy City,
the new Jerusalem, coming down out of heaven
from God, prepared as a bride beautifully dressed
for her husband. And I heard a loud voice from the
throne saying, 'Now the dwelling place of God is
with men and he will live with them. [Now notice
how this next sentence just drips with covenantal
terminology.] They will be his people, and God
himself will be with them and be their God. He will
wipe away every tear from their eyes. There will be
no more death or mourning or crying or pain
(Revelation 21:1-4).

When God says that the purpose of the covenant of
grace is to save us, what a tremendous salvation he
promises to give us!

Jesus is the Mediator of the covenant of grace.
God's great plan of salvation centres around Jesus. He
is presented in the Bible as the mediator of the covenant
of grace in the sense that he alone has the authority and
power to make the terms of the covenant real and valid.
In the Old Testament covenants, animal sacrifices and
the shedding of blood were always present. The
animal's blood ratified the covenant agreement,
making its terms valid and binding. For example, in
Exodus 24, when Moses had outlined the terms of the
covenant to God's people, he sprinkled them with
blood.

> Then Moses sent young Israelite men, and they
> offered burnt offerings and sacrificed young bulls as
> fellowship offerings to the LORD. Moses took half of
> the blood and put it in bowls, and the other half he
> sprinkled on the altar. Then he took the Book of the
> Covenant and read it to the people. They responded,
> 'We will do everything the LORD has said; we will
> obey.' Moses then took the blood, sprinkled it on
> the people and said, 'This is the blood of the
> covenant that the LORD has made with you in
> accordance with all these words.'

The sprinkled blood signified that the covenant
arrangements were valid and binding on the people.
   Jesus is the mediator of the covenant of grace
because his death, his shed blood, makes the covenant

terms real, valid and binding. For example, God promised he would forgive our sins. However, that promise could not become valid until Jesus had died because 'without the shedding of blood, there is no forgiveness' (Hebrews 9:22).

God also promised he would put his Holy Spirit within us. But that promise could not become real until Jesus had died. John 7:37-39 indicates:

> On the last and greatest day of the Feast, Jesus stood and said in a loud voice, 'If a man is thirsty, let him come to me and drink. Whoever believes in me, as the Scripture has said, streams of living water will flow within him.'

Then John himself makes the following comment:

> By this He meant the Spirit, whom those who believed in Him were to receive. Up to that time [the covenant promise of] the Spirit had not been given, since Jesus had not yet been glorified [and Jesus being glorified is a technical term for Jesus' death in John's Gospel].

It is clear, then, that Jesus is the mediator of the covenant of grace, making its promises valid and real and its terms binding by his death. Without his death, it would not have come into force.

Jesus is the focal point of the covenant of grace. The Old Testament, the old administration of the covenant, looked forward to Jesus. God's promise to Adam after his failure to keep the covenant of works pointed forward to Jesus, who would come as the last Adam and who, by his perfect obedience to God's law, would secure life for all those he represented.

In his covenant with Abraham, God had promised that 'all peoples on earth will be blessed through you' (Genesis 12:3), and that promise was fulfilled in Jesus. All the Old Testament sacrifices, religious festivals, all the rituals, all the prophecies, and all the institutions such as the priesthood pointed to Jesus and his death. Later in 2 Samuel 7:13-15, God made this promise to David about one of his descendants: 'I will establish his kingdom.... I will establish the throne of his kingdom forever. I will be his Father and he will be my son.... My love will never be taken away from him.' That promise was ultimately fulfilled in Jesus.

The Old Testament looked forward to Jesus, and the New Testament, the new administration of the covenant, states that Jesus the mediator has come.

Jesus himself saw his own death in covenantal terms, as implementing and ratifying the covenant of grace. Here is how he described his death:

> Then he [Jesus] took the cup, gave thanks and offered it to them, saying, 'Drink from it, all of you. This is my blood of the covenant, which is poured out for many for the forgiveness of sins' (Matthew 26:27-28).

The whole of the book of Hebrews revolves around the idea of the covenant of grace and Jesus as the mediator of the covenant. Without his death, without his shed blood, the covenant could not have come into force.

The covenant of grace lays certain obligations upon Christians.

Although God entered into covenant with us because he wanted to, and not on the basis of who we are or what we have done, God still requires us to respond to his initiative of grace. We have certain covenant obligations.

First of all, we must believe the covenant promises. By faith the benefits of the covenant become ours personally.

The Jews fell into the trap of thinking that the covenant promises became theirs automatically because they were born Jews, had been circumcised and tried to keep the law. Many people today fall into a similar trap. They think that because they have been born into a Christian family, have been baptised and do their best to live a decent life that they will enjoy God's salvation. But the Bible is at pains to point out that the salvation outlined in the covenant of grace becomes ours by faith alone. This is well-illustrated by the case of Abraham. He believed the LORD (Genesis 15:6). Abraham entered into an enjoyment of God's salvation because he believed the covenant promises. The same is true of us.

However, faith in the covenant promises leads, necessarily, to *obedience to the covenant regulations.* God summons those with whom he has entered into covenant and who have come to enjoy his salvation, to live in a certain way. We are to obey God so that glory is brought to him. This obedience is not optional, but obligatory. It is essential to the whole idea of the covenant of grace.

The Bible's teaching about how we are to live is

always set in a covenantal setting. Take the Ten Commandments. How do they begin? With a statement that is saturated with covenantal overtones: 'I am the LORD [Yahweh, God's covenant name] your God [another covenantal phrase], who [in fulfilment of my covenant with Abraham] brought you out of Egypt, out of the land of slavery.'

Our obedience to the Ten Commandments is not an attempt to earn God's salvation. It is our response of love to God's saving initiative.

Consider the passages in Ephesians 4-6 and Colossians 3-4, in which Paul sets out how Christians are to live. These passages have a covenantal structure to them. Paul does not begin these letters by telling us what we are to do. Instead, he spends time writing about God's salvation (Ephesians 1-3 and Colossians 1-2), and it is only after doing this that he tells us how we are to live. He is saying that our obedience is to be a loving response to what God has done for us in Jesus.

These are the obligations laid upon us by the covenant of grace. We are to believe the covenant promises and obey the covenant regulations. However, we can only do both by the power of the Holy Spirit. Unless the Spirit works in our hearts we cannot believe or obey. However, under the terms of the covenant of grace, God has promised us his Spirit to help us carry out our covenant obligations.

To summarise:

The covenant of grace is the unifying theme of the Bible, and undergirds the entire revelation of salvation. The need for the covenant of grace arose because of our sin. But God took the initiative, graciously promising that, through Jesus and on the basis of his death on the cross, he would save us. In response to all that he has done for us through Jesus, God wants us to believe the covenant promises and then to obey the covenant regulations. However this is only possible through the Holy Spirit's activity in our lives.

It would be natural, perhaps, to say at this junction: 'I thought that this book was about baptism. But so far it is all about the covenant of grace.' We need to be patient, however.

The covenant of grace is the basis for our understanding of baptism. In fact, everything I say about baptism will stem from this idea of the covenant of grace. If the builder mentioned at the start of this chapter had been more patient and put in solid foundations, the bungalow he built would be occupied today instead of standing derelict and uninhabited. Let us make sure we have the foundation right. Then we can move on to other matters.

References

1. Westminster Confession of Faith, Chapter 7 Section I.
2. *The Shorter Catechism*, Question 16.
3. *Ibid.*, Question 19

THE MEANING OF BAPTISM

Several years ago, I was talking to a lady, who was a Quaker. Quakers do not baptize anyone, and they are also peace loving people. This lady said to me, 'Baptism causes such controversy between Christians. I think everyone would be better off doing what we do and baptising no-one.' Then she asked me, 'Why do you Presbyterians baptize at all?' How would you have answered her?

I hope you would have replied that we baptize because Jesus instructed us to do so. When Jesus met with his disciples in Galilee after his resurrection, he said to them, 'All authority in heaven and on earth has been given to me. Therefore go and make disciples of all nations, baptising them in the name of the Father and of the Son and of the Holy Spirit' (Matthew 28:18-19). We baptize not because we think it is a good idea, or because it is something the church has always done, but because Jesus told us to and we want to obey him. We are sad that baptism causes such controversy between Christians, but we cannot stop baptising; otherwise we will be guilty of disobeying Jesus' clear command.

Granted that baptism was instituted by Jesus himself, what is it?

Baptism is an indication of admission to the visible church.

When it speaks about 'the church', the Bible makes three important distinctions. First, the Bible distinguishes between the *militant* church and the *triumphant* church. The militant church is the church on earth, which engages in spiritual warfare against the world, the flesh and the devil. The triumphant church is the church in heaven, which has overcome its spiritual opponents.

Secondly, the Bible distinguishes between the *universal* church and the *local* church. The universal church is made up of Christians from every nation throughout the earth. The local church is made up of Christians in one particular locality. We often use the word 'congregation' when referring to the local church.

Thirdly, the Bible distinguishes between the *invisible* church and the *visible* church. This distinction applies to the church as it exists on earth. The invisible church is made up of those whom God has chosen, so it is impossible to say precisely who do and who do not make up the invisible church. Only God knows. The visible church, on the other hand, is made up of people who outwardly profess faith in Christ. Whether, in reality, they are saved is impossible to determine. However, they are members of the visible church because they outwardly say that they believe in Jesus Christ and, at the present, give evidence that their profession of faith is credible.

Through baptism, we were brought into the fellowship of the visible church. That is not to say that being baptised makes you a Christian. We do not believe that because the Bible does not teach that. Not everyone who is in the fellowship of the visible church is saved.

Good and evil will always be found together in the professing church until the end of the world. Thus J. C. Ryle notes: 'The visible church is ... a mixed body. ... We must expect to find believers and unbelievers, converted and unconverted, ... all mingled together in every congregation of baptised people.'[1]

The only people who are saved are those who are part of the invisible church, and we become part of the invisible church, not through baptism, but through turning from our sin, trusting in Jesus as our Saviour and following him as our Lord. Being baptised does not make anyone a Christian, but it does bring us into the fellowship of God's people in the visible church.

Baptism as the mark of admission into the visible church is clearly taught in the Bible. Under the old administration of the covenant of grace in Old Testament times, circumcision was the mark of the people with whom God had entered into covenant. God commanded Abraham to circumcise himself as an indication that he had entered into covenant with him: 'You are to undergo circumcision, and it will be a sign of the covenant between me and you' (Genesis 17:11). God issued a warning that any male who was not circumcised was not part of the fellowship of God's people: 'Any uncircumcised male, who has not been circumcised in the flesh, will be cut off from his people. He has broken my covenant' (Genesis 17:14).

Thus in Old Testament times, circumcision was the mark that indicated admission into the visible church. 'Contrary to the general practice of the nations at large, circumcision for Israel is not to be a sign of introduction to manhood,'[2] because it was eight-day-old boys who were to be circumcised. Also, because God told Abraham that he was to circumcise 'those born in your household or bought with money from a foreigner – those who are not your offspring'[3], 'from the day of its original institution, ... circumcision was open to the gentiles [and] was not intended exclusively as a racial badge'.[4]

If circumcision did not signify the arrival of manhood and if it was not a racial badge, what did it signify? 'Circumcision symbolised inclusion in the covenant community.'[5] Now, arguing from the fact that under the new administration of the covenant of grace, in what we call New Testament times, circumcision has been replaced by water baptism, we can say that today baptism is the indication that a person is part of the fellowship of God's people, the community related to God by covenant.

This link between circumcision and membership of the visible church is carried through into the New Testament. In the New Testament, it was baptism that marked people off as being members of the visible church (see 1 Corinthians 12:13; Galatians 3:27-28; Acts 2:41; Acts 10:44-48). Notice the sequence in Acts 2:41: 'Those who accepted the message were baptised, and about three thousand were added to their number that day.' Repentance and faith in Jesus by people who have not been previously baptised, leads to baptism, which leads to admission to the visible church. It is through baptism that we are brought within the fellowship of God's people, the visible church.

It is important to stress this because some Christians tend to divorce baptism and admission into the fellowship of God's people. They are prepared to baptize people without incorporating them into the visible church. The Bible does not do this, so neither should we. Those we baptize are admitted into the fellowship of God's people. It is vitally important for the baptised believer to be part of the fellowship of God's people, because it is within the context of the visible church, with its preaching of God's Word and administration of the sacraments and opportunities for service, that the Christian's faith is strengthened.

Baptism is a sign of the covenant of grace.

What biblical evidence is there for the idea of baptism being a sign of the covenant of grace? The main strand of biblical evidence concerns the replacement of circumcision, as the sign of the covenant, by baptism.

Under the old administration of the covenant of grace, circumcision was the sign of the covenant. Paul says as much in Romans 4:11: Abraham 'received the sign of circumcision'. In Colossians 2:11-12, Paul indicates that baptism has taken the place of circumcision as the sign of the covenant. It is true that, in this passage, Paul has in mind spiritual realities, circumcision of the heart and baptism by the Spirit, rather than physical circumcision and baptism. However, as Harry Uprichard argues:

> If Paul identifies the inner realities of which physical circumcision and water baptism are the outer signs, it is reasonable to assume that he identified the outer signs too. It would have been exceedingly difficult for him to write in this particular fashion had he not.[6]

If baptism has replaced circumcision, just as the Lord's Supper has replaced the Passover, then baptism must be reckoned to be, like circumcision, namely, a sign of the covenant of grace.

Now what do we mean when we say that baptism is a sign of the covenant of grace?

What is a sign? It is something visible that points away from itself to a reality different and more significant than itself. As a motorist drives along the road, he sees a sign for London. The function of that sign is to point the motorist in the direction of London. The city of London is very different in reality from the sign. No-one would ever mix up a metal sign and the city of London! As the largest city in England, London is much more significant than a sign by the side of the road.

Baptism is a sign, in that it is visible – we see water being poured or sprinkled on someone, but it points away from itself to something far more significant. It focuses our attention on God's salvation in the covenant of grace.

If you like things packaged in more theological terms, a sign is something 'which, commencing from sensible things, according to a predetermined analogy, [is] designed by God to display and explain to us, by making them more clear, those benefits which are invisible and eternal'.[7] Baptism is a sign of the covenant of grace because the water used in baptism, which is something visible and sensible, displays and points us to invisible and eternal spiritual realities, namely, God's salvation in Jesus.

As a sign, baptism tells us what the salvation God offers under the terms of the covenant of grace is like.

In Scripture, the symbol of washing with water and the idea of baptism are linked with:

1. Cleansing from sin: 'I will sprinkle clean water on you, and you will be clean. I will cleanse you from all your impurities and from all your idols' (Ezekiel 36:25).

2. Forgiveness of sins: 'Repent and be baptised, every one of you, in the name of Jesus Christ, so that your sins may be forgiven' (Acts 2:38).

3. Union with Christ: 'Do you not know that all of us who were baptised into Christ Jesus were baptised into his death?' (Romans 6:3).

4. Adoption: 'You are all sons of God through faith in Christ Jesus, for all of you who were baptised into Christ have been clothed with Christ' (Galatians 3:26-27).

5. The new birth: Jesus links being 'born again' with being 'born of water' (John 3:3, 5).

6. The gift of the Holy Spirit: 'I will sprinkle clean water on you. ... I will give you a new heart. ... I will put my Spirit in you and move you to follow my decrees' (Ezekiel 36:25-27).

7. The resurrection to eternal life: 'If we have been united with him in his death [something signified by baptism], we will certainly also be united with him in his resurrection' (Romans 6:5).

What is the salvation God offers under the arrangements of the covenant of grace like? Baptism tells us. It points to the fact that God's salvation is absolutely wonderful and complete. Baptism tells us that when God saves someone, he regenerates that person, so that he can turn from his sin and place his trust in Jesus. When the person repents and believes, he finds that God forgives his sins, cleanses him from the inward defilement caused by sin, brings him into his family, unites him to Jesus and puts his Holy Spirit in his heart so that he has the spiritual strength to please God and to obey his Word. Then, when he dies, God takes that person to be with him in heaven for all eternity and, at the resurrection, gives him a new resurrection body.

The salvation which baptism points to is all-embracing. It covers the whole of a person's spiritual experience – from regeneration, to justification and adoption, to sanctification, and right through to glorification. Sometimes people accuse us of making far too much of baptism. We cannot help it. Look at the wonderful and complete salvation it signifies! Is it any wonder we make much of baptism? We love to speak about it because it tells us about the great salvation God has secured for his people on the basis of Jesus' death.

A point of division

It is here that baptists (who baptize only those who profess faith) and paedobaptists (those who baptize believers and their children) part company.

Baptists believe baptism is a sign that the person baptised has faith in Jesus. They say that baptism is something done by the believer. A. H. Strong, a famous

Baptist theologian, wrote that baptism is 'declaring a previous spiritual change in him who submits to it'.[8] He adds that baptism is 'strictly ... an ... act on the part of the believer'.[9] Generally speaking, baptists insist that baptism is a sign of man's faith. What Scripture stresses, however, is that baptism is a sign of God's grace. Baptism points to what God has done for us, and not what we have done for God. It is an outward sign of the salvation God promises to the person who believes in Jesus as Saviour and Lord, and not an outward sign that the person baptised has believed in Jesus as Saviour and Lord.

A clear understanding that baptism is a sign of the covenant of grace, and not a sign of a person's faith, provides the answer to one of the most common baptist objections to the practice of baptising believers' children. 'Infant baptism is wrong,' baptists will say, 'because children are too young to repent and believe.' Sometimes other Christians are unduly disturbed by this criticism, until they realise that behind that objection lies a misunderstanding of what baptism is. The objection assumes that baptism is a sign of faith. It is not. It is a sign of God's grace. If baptism was a sign of faith, then repentance and faith would be necessary before baptism is administered, and the Baptists' objection would be valid. However, because it is a sign of God's grace, pointing to God's salvation, the objection is invalid.

Baptism is a seal of the Covenant of Grace.

In Romans 4:11, Paul not only describes circumcision as a 'sign', but he says that it was also 'a seal of the righteousness that he [Abraham] had by faith'. On the basis that circumcision is the Old Testament equivalent to baptism, we can say that baptism is a seal of the covenant of grace, of God's salvation.

What is a seal? Let me say right away that it is not the same as a sign. 'It is more than a sign of spiritual blessing.'[10] Often this difference is not recognised. So what is the difference between a seal and a sign? Pierre Marcel is helpful:

> Seals are distinct from signs in that they not only reminds us of invisible things, but also authenticate these things to our religious consciousness by making them more certain and sure to us.[11]

Palmer Robertson makes the same point, if in a more homely way:

> A down payment – a notarized signature – a handshake – a kiss. Any of these actions may seal a promise. A man is as good as his word, but it's nice to have an action to seal the understanding communicated by the word. So God also made a way for reassurance. We ought to know that God's word is good. He cannot lie. But the weakness of human faith welcomes an act of reassurance.[12]

Baptism, as a seal, is given to reassure us of the reality of God's grace and visually to confirm and guarantee a spoken promise. The New Testament Greek word which is translated by the English word 'seal' means, in modern Greek, an engagement ring. This throws light on what a seal is. When a couple get engaged, they make promises to each other that, one day, they will get married. Everyone knows that these spoken promises have been made because the girl appears with an engagement ring on the third finger of her left hand. That engagement ring acts like a seal, visually confirming a spoken promise. If the girl ever doubted that her fiancé had proposed to her, all she would have to do is look at her engagement ring, and it would confirm her fiancé's spoken promise that, one day, they would be husband and wife.

In the same way, baptism is a seal of the covenant of grace. It helps us in our weakness. God's promises are trustworthy, but sometimes we sinfully doubt his promises. In his goodness towards us, God has given us baptism as a visual confirmation of the promises of salvation that he has made to us. Just as the rainbow visually confirmed to Noah the genuineness of God's spoken promise that he would never again destroy the world by means of a flood, so baptism visually confirms to us the genuineness of God's promises of salvation in Jesus.

This idea of baptism as a seal of the covenant of grace has far-reaching implications.

Baptism, as a seal of the covenant of grace, reassures Christians that they are recipients of God's salvation.

The historical circumstances surrounding the introduction of circumcision as a seal of the covenant indicate this.

In Genesis 15, God came to Abraham and promised him salvation. Abraham took God at his word and was justified. God, then, appeared to Abraham in what one writer has called 'one of the most spectacular divine revelations recorded in human history'.[13] However, in Genesis 16, there follows the sordid incident involving Abraham and Hagar, when Abraham failed miserably to trust in God. Abraham's faith was at an all-time low.

Then, in Genesis 17, God came to Abraham again and repeated his promises of salvation to him. God wanted to give Abraham something which would confirm to him that he was still loved by God and which would reassure him that his sin had not disqualified him from receiving God's promises. This time God did not give Abraham a vision, a spectacular spiritual experience. Instead he gave the sign of circumcision as 'the seal of the righteousness he had by faith' (Romans 4:11). It was not an extravagant spiritual experience that was going to confirm to Abraham that he was a recipient of God's promises of salvation – it was circumcision, the seal of the covenant.

It is the same for Christians. There are times when Christians doubt their salvation. They wonder if they really are the recipients of God's salvation. Many Christians who lack assurance long for some spectacular spiritual experience that will confirm to them that God does love them. They never get one, because that is not how God works. He does give them confirmation that he loves them, but it is not in some extravagant spiritual experience. It is in the sacraments, those signs and seals of God's salvation on the basis of Jesus' death. In his *Institutes of the Christian Religion*, John Calvin writes this about the sacraments as seals of the covenant of grace:

The believer, when he sees the sacraments with his own eyes, does not halt at the physical sight of them, but ... rises up in devout contemplation of those lofty mysteries which lie hidden in the sacraments.[14]

Christians should daily remember their baptism as a seal of the promises God has made to them. If they constantly recalled the meaning of their baptism, they would never doubt that God loves them and that they are recipients of his promises of salvation.

So what is baptism? According to the Bible, it is an indication of admission into the visible church, a sign of the covenant of grace, and a seal of the covenant of grace. Do not settle for anything less.

References
1. J. C. Ryle, *Expository Thoughts on the Gospels – Matthew* (Welwyn, England: Evangelical Press, 1977), 146-147.
2. O. Palmer Robertson, *The Christ of the Covenants* (Phillipsburg, New Jersey: Presbyterian and Reformed Publishing Company, 1980), 149.
3. Genesis 17:12.
4. Robertson, *The Christ of the Covenants*, 149.
5. *Ibid.*, 150.
6. R.E.H. Uprichard, *Baptism* (Belfast, Northern Ireland: Westminster Fellowship Trust, 1980), 19.
7. Pierre Ch. Marcel, *The Biblical Doctrine of Infant Baptism*, trans. Philip Edgcumbe Hughes (London: James Clarke and Company Limited, 1953), 29.
8. Augustus H. Strong, *Systematic Theology* (London: Pickering and Inglis Limited, 1906), 946.
9. Strong, 948.

10. Marcel, 30.
11. *Ibid*.
12. O Palmer Robertson, *Covenants: God's Way With His People* (Philadelphia: Great Commission Publications, 1987), 51.
13. Robertson, *Ibid*, 51.
14. John Calvin, *Institutes of the Christian Religion*. Ed. by John T. McNeill. Trans. by Ford Lewis Battles. (Philadelphia: The Westminster Press, 1960), IV.XIV.5.

3

THE SUBJECTS OF BAPTISM

I was once asked to speak to a group of young adults about baptism. I began by asking them this question: Whom do Presbyterians believe should be baptised? One of them immediately replied, 'That is easy! Presbyterians believe in infant baptism.' But in fact that is not exactly what Presbyterians (or other paedobaptists) believe. The *Westminster Confession of Faith* says this about the subjects of baptism: 'Not only those who profess faith in and obedience to Christ are to be baptised, but also the infants of one or both believing parents.'[1] Two groups of people should be baptised – adults not previously baptised who have become Christians, and the children of Christians.

Does the Bible teach that adults, not previously baptised but who have become Christians, should be baptised?

Clearly the answer to that question is 'Yes!' In Old Testament times, when a Gentile adult male wanted to become a Jew, he was circumcised, and circumcision, as we have argued, is the Old Testament equivalent of baptism. In New Testament times, when someone who had not been baptised became a Christian, he was baptised. In this connection we can think of the three thousand people who became Christians on the Day of Pentecost, or individuals as the Ethiopian Eunuch, Lydia, and the Philippian Jailer. These people had never been baptised, but, after they believed in Jesus, they were. The Bible clearly teaches that adults, not previously baptised but who have become Christians, should be baptised.

But does not a verse such as Acts 2:38 contradict this last statement? In fact it causes us no embarrassment. Those people on the Day of Pentecost, to whom that command was addressed, had not been previously baptised. When they became Christians, it was proper to baptize them. When adults, who have never been baptised before, become Christians, paedobaptists are delighted to baptize them. If anyone says to us, 'I have just become a Christian but I have never been baptised, will you baptize me?', every paedobaptist minister would be more than happy to do so! As a Presbyterian minister, I have baptised adults on their own profession of faith.

Are you beginning to get the picture? Paedobaptists do not just believe in baptising children. We believe that adults, who have not been previously baptised, but who have become Christians, should also be baptised.

Does the Bible teach that the children of Christians should be baptised?

It is over the practice of baptising the children of Christians that paedobaptists and Baptists[2] begin to part company. Paedobaptists believe the Bible also teaches that the children of Christians should be baptised. Baptists disagree. Paedobaptists do not believe all infants should be baptised, but only 'the infants of one or both believing parents'.[3] We also maintain that we can produce biblical data to back up our point-of-view on baptism.

1. The argument from the Covenant of Grace.

The main reason why we maintain that the baptism of believers' children is biblical is because of inferences which can be drawn from the Bible's teaching about the covenant of grace. The *Westminster Confession of Faith* states:

> The whole purpose of God about everything pertaining to his own glory and to man's salvation, faith and life is either explicitly stated in the Bible or may be deduced as inevitably and logically following from it.[3]

Our point-of-view about who should be baptised can be 'deduced as inevitably and logically following from' the Bible's teaching about the covenant of grace.

Now it is inconsistent of baptists to reject this method of biblical interpretation and say they will not accept pacdobaptism as biblical until chapter and verse can be cited, because they use exactly the same method of inference from the Bible's teaching to support other fundamental doctrines. For example, baptists also believe that God is triune. However, they arrive at that correct conclusion, not by being able to quote chapter and verse – because there is not a single verse in the Bible that explicitly states that God is triune – but by correct inference from the Bible's teaching. If they use that method of biblical interpretation to arrive at the doctrine of the Trinity, surely it is inconsistent to deny paedobaptists the right to use it to arrive at their doctrine of baptism?

So how do inferences drawn from the Bible's teaching about the covenant of grace point to the correctness of our point-of-view on baptism? In order to answer that question, we need to look at Genesis 17:1-14.

Notice several facts about these verses. First of all, God established his covenant. As the very start of Genesis 17:7 indicates, it was God who took the initiative and established this covenant: 'I will establish my covenant.' This covenant was not to do with land. It had to do with salvation because, at the end of Genesis 17:8, we find the covenantal catch-phrase 'I will be their God'. As we have seen, this phrase is an umbrella term to cover all the promises God makes in the covenant of grace such as union with Jesus in his death and resurrection, forgiveness and cleansing, justification, the indwelling Spirit and the hope of heaven.

Now with whom did God establish his covenant? God established his covenant with Abraham. Look at Genesis 17:7 again: 'I will establish my covenant ... between me and you ... to be your God.' What was Abraham's spiritual status before God entered into covenant with him? We are told, in Genesis 15:6, that he was a believer. God promised him he would have a son. Abraham believed God's promise, and, as a result of his faith, Abraham became right with God: 'Abraham believed the LORD, and he credited it [Abraham's faith] to him as righteousness.' So the covenant of Genesis 17 was made with a believer.

Did God establish his covenant only with Abraham? No, because Genesis 17:7 adds that God also established his covenant with Abraham's children: 'I will establish my covenant ... between me and you and your descendants after you for generations to come, to be your God and the God of your descendants after you.'

What was the spiritual status of Abraham's descendants? They were children of a believer. So, on the basis of Abraham's faith, God entered into covenant with Abraham's children. The believer's children were included within the covenant on the basis of the believer's faith.

Some people might find that strange, but I do not. I am a British citizen. However, I am a British citizen for a different reason from the vast majority of British citizens. They are British citizens because they were born in the United Kingdom. I was not. I was born in Nigeria, when my parents were missionaries there. So why am I a British citizen and not a Nigerian citizen? Because my father is a British citizen. On the basis of his British citizenship, I am a British citizen. In the same way, on the basis of the believer's faith, the believer's children are included within the covenant.

How did Abraham and his descendants know God had entered into covenant with them? God gave a sign to show that he had established his covenant with Abraham and his descendants. That sign was circumcision. This is recorded in Genesis 17:10-11:

'This is my covenant with you and your descendants after you, the covenant you are to keep: every male among you shall be circumcised. You are to undergo circumcision, and it will be the sign of the covenant between me and you.'

Every time Abraham or one of his male descendants realised he was circumcised, he would remember how

God had entered into covenant with him.

What has all this got to do with baptism? These covenant arrangements still operate today. We see in Genesis 17:7 how this covenant is described: 'I will establish my covenant as an everlasting covenant.' That the covenant which God made with Abraham and his descendants is an everlasting one is 'the assumption of the rest of the Old Testament',[4] and this theme is taken up in the New Testament. For example, in Hebrews 13:20, it is called 'the eternal covenant'.

The fact that God's covenant is everlasting and eternal implies that the covenant arrangements God established with Abraham are still the same today. God promises us the same salvation that he promised Abraham, and on the same basis – faith in Jesus. Just as he did in Abraham's time, God makes these promises to the believer and the believer's children.

The sign of the covenant is to be administered to the same people as it was in Abraham's time, namely to the believer and the believer's children. The only change is that, in keeping with the fact that the new administration of the covenant of grace is broader in its application than the old administration of the covenant of grace, baptism has replaced circumcision as the sign of the covenant. This means that females, as well as males, can receive it.

The main argument that paedobaptists put forward for the baptism of believers' children is the continuity of the covenant of grace in the Old and New Testaments.

If the people of God are the same in both dispensations, and the sacraments the same in substance, then the children included in the Old

Testament by the rite of circumcision are certainly not excluded in the New Testament from the equivalent rite of baptism.[5]

Under the old administration, because God's promise was 'to you and your seed' (Genesis 17:7), the covenant mark of circumcision was administered to believers' male children. This principle of 'to you and your seed' still operates under the new administration. 'This is the foundation of our understanding of the appropriateness of the application of baptism to our infant seed – the continuity involved in the covenant of God.'[6] Therefore the covenant mark, which is now baptism, should be administered to believers' children.

Baptists object to this and accuse paedobaptists of failing to grasp the radical difference between the old and new administrations of the covenant. They argue that the principle of 'to you and your seed' (which forms the basis for the justification of the baptism of believers' children) no longer operates in the new covenant. However, the interesting thing is that it is often precisely in the context of emphasising the differences between the old and new covenants that the continuity of the principle 'to you and your seed' is underlined. Take, for example, Peter's sermon on the Day of Pentecost. As he explains Joel 2:28-32, Peter spells out the differences between the old and new administrations of the covenant. In particular, he says that the covenant promise of the Spirit is not restricted to the Messianic figures of the Old Testament – the prophet, the priest and the king – but he has been poured out on all flesh. Peter describes how the new covenant has now arrived.

Then, in the context of spelling out the differences

between the old and new administrations, Peter emphasises that there is one factor that continues on from the old into the new, and it is that the covenant promise is 'for you and your children and for all who are far off – for all whom the Lord our God will call' (Acts 2:39).

Peter stresses that, with the arrival of the new, many old covenantal patterns have been destroyed. However, there is one old covenantal pattern which has not been destroyed and which will be carried on under the new covenant, namely, the promise is not only to believers but also to their children. In the context of outlining the differences between the old and new covenants, Peter explicitly underlines the fact that the principle of 'to you and your seed' has not been done away with in the new covenant. The New Testament itself shows that this criticism of the main reason why we baptize believers' children is invalid.

The baptism of believers' children does not rest upon the tradition that paedobaptists have always done it this way, or on a few isolated Bible texts drawn from here and there. It is based upon legitimate inferences drawn from the Bible's teaching about the covenant of grace, the great unifying and central theme of the whole of God's Word. On the basis of the covenant of grace, we believe it is biblical and reasonable to hold that not only adults, not previously baptised but who have become Christians, should be baptised, but also the children of Christians have the right to receive the covenant sign of baptism.

2. The argument from the nature of the church.
All who are members of the visible church have the right to the privileges of church membership, and those privileges include participation in the sacraments. Who, then, is a member of the visible church? According to baptists, the visible church is 'a company of regenerate persons'.[7] This is why they only baptize people who profess to be Christians. However, paedobaptists maintain that the Bible teaches that the visible church is made up of 'all those throughout the world that profess the true religion *and of their children*'[8] (italics added). In both the Old Testament and the New Testament, the children of believers were regarded as being an integral part of the visible church. For example, one of the Ten Commandments – the Fifth Commandment – is specifically directed towards children. Also Paul addressed sections of his letters expressly to children. If the sacraments are the right of the members of the visible church and if believers' children are part of the visible church, then they have the right to be baptised.

3. The argument that baptism is the right of all who belong to the kingdom of God.
Jesus himself makes it clear that believers' children belong to God's kingdom. He said, 'Let the little children come to me ... for the kingdom of God belongs to such as these' (Luke 18:16). Baptists argue that Jesus is not saying these little children, the children of believers, belong to the kingdom, but that those who are like children belong to the kingdom.

That line of reasoning is invalid because, consistently in the New Testament, the Greek word which is translated 'such as' introduces a category and not a comparison. It is always used 'in such a way that a definite individual [or group] with special characteristics is thought of'.[9] For example, it is used in Galatians 6:1 to refer to the person who is caught up in a sin; in Titus 3:11 to those who cause divisions among Christians; and in 2 Corinthians 10:11 to those stirring up trouble for Paul in Corinth. When Jesus uses the phrase 'such as' in connection with the children of believers in Luke 18:16, he is saying that this category belong to God's kingdom. If baptism is the right of all who belong to the kingdom of God, then believers' children have the right to baptism.

4. The argument from the examples of household baptism in the New Testament.

Baptists claim there are no examples of infants being baptised in the New Testament. But that is not necessarily the case. In the New Testament, there are three examples of household baptism. In Acts 16:15, we are told that Lydia and 'the members of her household were baptised'. In Acts 16:33, the Philippian jailer and 'all his family were baptised'. In 1 Corinthians 1:15, Paul tells that he 'baptised the household of Stephanas'. While admitting that the Bible does not say Lydia's household, the Philippian Jailer's family and Stephanas' household contained children, it does not say they did not. In fact, it is quite probable that they did. While these three examples of household baptism do not prove conclusively that the early church baptised the infants of believers, they do give grounds to question the baptist claim that there are no examples of infants being baptised in the New Testament.

5. The argument from the silence of the New Testament.

Often those who do not agree with our point-of-view on baptism will say, 'Show me a single verse in the New Testament which states clearly that children of believers were baptised.' We have to concede that we cannot. The New Testament is silent about this matter. But, far from this silence demolishing our position on baptism, we believe that the New Testament's silence actually supports our position.

Why is the New Testament silent about this matter? Because the baptism of children of Christians was taken so much for granted, there was no need for it to be specifically mentioned. Baptising the infants of believers was so much the norm for the early church it was never challenged, and so the writers of the New Testament never had any cause to mention it. Far from undermining our point-of-view on baptism, we believe that the silence of the New Testament actually supports our position.

Notice that this argument from the silence of the New Testament cuts both ways. Baptists say to us, 'You cannot show us a single verse in the New Testament that clearly states that children of believers were baptised.' However, we could, with equal validity, ask them to show us a single verse in the New Testament which states clearly that children of Christians were baptised as adults. They cannot point to one. One writer has put it this way:

There are in the New Testament decidedly fewer traces, indeed none at all, of the baptism of adults born of parents already Christian and brought up by them.... Those who dispute the biblical character of infant baptism have ... to reckon with the fact that adult baptism of sons and daughters born of Christian parents, which they recommend, is even worse attested by the New Testament than infant baptism ... and indeed lacks any kind of proof.[10]

The silence of the New Testament cuts both ways.

This argument from the silence of the New Testament should not be played down. Some baptists are extremely sceptical about this way of arguing without realising they do exactly the same thing about other issues. For example, both paedobaptists and baptists allow women to take part in the Lord's Supper. Yet there is not one single verse in the New Testament which shows clearly that women did take part in the Lord's Supper in the early church. However, both paedobaptists and baptists reason from silence that it is God's will for women to take part in the Lord's Supper, and say the New Testament is silent because this was just taken for granted. It is therefore a little inconsistent for baptists to use the argument from silence to support the way they administer one sacrament, but not to allow paedobaptists to use it to support the way we administer the other one.

Baptism, as a seal of the covenant of grace, reminds Christian parents that their child belongs to God in a special way.

In Ephesians 1:13, Paul describes the Holy Spirit as a seal guaranteeing Christians that they belong to Jesus. When children receive the seal of baptism, they are marked out as belonging to Jesus in a special way, to be the recipient of God's salvation. One writer has put it this way:

> The baptism of a child means that the stamp of being God's property has been put on the child in a public way, that the child ... is openly claimed by God for a destiny of salvation.[11]

In baptism, God assures Christian parents that the covenant God has made with them in Christ is also made with their children.

When God made a covenant with Noah, he gave him a promise of salvation, namely, he would never destroy the world by means of a flood. God pointed to the rainbow in the sky as a sign of that covenant. The interesting thing is that, according to Genesis 9:16, whenever he sees a rainbow, God remembers his covenant promises. The sign of the covenant causes God to remember his promises to whose with whom he has entered into covenant.

In the Bible, the idea of God remembering does not mean that he has forgotten. He is all-knowing and never suffers from amnesia. But God's remembering does indicate a mental activity on his part. He brings the matter to the forefront of his thinking. It also suggests an act of his will: 'When God remembers, he does something. He takes action, either in blessing, as in Psalm 115:12, or in judgment, as in Jeremiah 14:10.'[12] In a similar way, baptism, the sign of the covenant, causes God to remember the believer's child. He brings to the forefront of his thinking the promises of salvation he made to that child, and he acts in blessing towards the believer's child, actively seeking to bring him or her into a personal commitment to himself through faith in Jesus. The believer's child's baptism is a visual confirmation of these promises made by God.

This does not mean that the believer's child will automatically become a Christian. He or she still will have to commit themselves to Jesus as they grow up. The idea of the engagement ring illustrates this. When a couple get engaged, they are still not married. They might have been told about some of the joys of married life, yet they have not personally experienced them. They will not experience married life until they commit themselves to each other on their wedding day. A child does not become a Christian just because he or she was baptised. In baptism, they are engaged to be the Lord's. They, while knowing about God's salvation, will not personally experience it until they commit themselves to God through faith in Jesus.

References

1. *Westminster Confession of Faith*, Chapter 28, Section IV.
2. By baptists I do not simply mean Baptist denominations. I mean all those who maintain that baptism should only be administered to adults who profess faith in Jesus and that it should be carried out by immersion.
3. *Westminster Confession of Faith*, Chapter 28, Section IV.
4. Gordon Wenham, *Genesis 16-50* (Dallas, Texas: Word Books, 1994), 30.
5. John H. Gerstner, Douglas F. Kelly and Philip Rollinson, *A Guide to the Westminster Confession of Faith* (Signal Mountain, Tennessee: Summertown Texts, 1992), 142-143.
6. Sinclair B. Ferguson, *The Theology of Infant Baptism*,

Audiotape lecture given to the Westminster Fellowship, October 1991, Tape 1 Side 2.

7. Strong, 945.

8. *Westminster Confession of Faith*, Chapter 25, Section II.

9. William F. Arndt and F. Wilbur Gingrich, *A Greek-English Lexicon of the New Testament* (Cambridge, England: Cambridge University Press, 1957), 829.

10. Oscar Cullmann, *Baptism in the New Testament*, trans. J. K. S. Reid (London: SCM Press Limited, 1950), 26.

11. P. T. Forsyth; quoted in James Philip, *The Westminster Confession of Faith: An Exposition, vol. 2* (Didasko Press, 1984), 134.

12. John W. Sanderson, *Mirrors of His Glory* (Phillipsburg, New Jersey: Presbyterian and Reformed Publishing Company, 1991), 24.

CHAPTER 4

THE MODE OF BAPTISM

Dr. Harry Uprichard begins his short book on baptism with this statement: 'Of all the subjects within the Christian church, baptism is one of the most controversial.'[1] While that is certainly true, it is also true to say that, of all the aspects of this controversial subject, the mode of baptism is possibly the most contentious. Some very bitter and acrimonious debates have taken place between Christians as to how baptism should be administered.

When it comes to the mode of baptism, there are basically three competing views. At one end of the spectrum, there is the view that immersion is the only mode: 'The command to baptize is a command to immerse.'[2] Then, at the other end of the spectrum, is the conviction that sprinkling or pouring is the preferable mode of baptism. As the *Westminster Confession of Faith* puts it: 'Baptism is correctly administered by pouring or sprinkling water on the person.'[3] Finally, there is, what we may call, the halfway house point-of-view. Those who hold this position believe that either pouring or sprinkling or immersion will do. They maintain that, 'so long as water is used in the name of the Trinity, the precise mode of administering the ordinance is left an open question.'[4] They even appeal to the Westminster Confession for support because it states that immersion is not forbidden but simply 'not necessary'.[5]

In what follows we will argue that sprinkling or pouring, and not immersion or both immersion and pouring or sprinkling, is the mode of baptism taught in the Bible.

The case for baptism by immersion is not proven.
The case for immersion rests upon three claims: (1) the Greek verbs *baptizo* and *bapto*, from which we obviously get our English word 'baptism', always means to immerse; (2) the New Testament's description of some baptisms implies immersion; (3) what baptism symbolises is only expressed by immersion.

If we examine each of these, we will discover that none of them necessarily teaches immersion.

1. The Greek verbs *baptizo* and *bapto* always means to immerse.

Baptists contend that 'the command to baptize is a command to immerse'.[6] This assertion is based on the claim that the Greek words *bapto* and *baptizo* always mean to immerse. '*Baptizo* in the whole history of the Greek language has but one [meaning]. It not only signifies to ... immerse, but it never has any other meaning.'[7] However, their claim that *bapto* and *baptizo* always mean to immerse is not as well-founded as is suggested.

The verb *bapto* is the one mainly used in the Septuagint, the Greek translation of the Old Testament. In Leviticus 11:32 and Job 9:31 it probably means to immerse. Yet what determines its meaning in these two cases is not the mere use of *bapto* but the context in which it is found. However, there are numerous instances where the Septuagint's use of *bapto* makes the baptist claim unreasonable.

Here is one example. In Leviticus 14:6 and Leviticus 14:51 details are given of the ritual to be used in the cleansing of a leper and of a house in which leprosy has occurred. The priest is to take some cedar wood, scarlet yarn, hyssop and a live bird, and dip them in the blood of another bird that had been killed. The verb used is *bapto* and, if it always means to immerse, then the live bird was submerged in the blood of the dead bird. Surely this is improbable.

There are other examples in the Old Testament which show that *bapto* does not necessarily mean to immerse: Exodus 12:12; Leviticus 4:6; Leviticus 4:17; Leviticus 9:9; Leviticus 14:15-16; Numbers 19:18; Deuteronomy 33:24; Ruth 2:14; 1 Samuel 14:27; Daniel 4:30; Daniel 5:21.

In the New Testament *baptizo* is used rather than *bapto*, yet the same pattern emerges. *Baptizo* does not always mean to immerse. Take, for example, 1 Corinthians 10:3. Paul writes that the Israelites 'were baptised into Moses in the cloud and in the sea'. Paul's statement cannot mean that the Israelites were immersed in the cloud and the sea. It was the Egyptians, and not the Israelites, who were drowned by being immersed in the Red Sea. Neither did the Israelites immerse themselves in the cloud. The cloud came upon them. Whatever the verb *baptizo* means in 1 Corinthians 10:3, it does not mean to immerse.

Another example of an instance where it is incorrect to suggest that *baptizo* can only mean to immerse is Luke 11:38. Jesus had been invited to dinner at an unnamed Pharisee's house. The Pharisee was surprised to find 'that Jesus did not wash before the meal'. The verb used is *baptizo*, and it refers to Jewish ceremonial washings. Sometimes these involved washing up to the wrist and sometimes up to the elbow, but they never involved a complete bath, which a meaning of immerse for *baptizo* would require.

Not only does the New Testament's use of *baptizo* not necessarily imply immersion, but in Hebrews 9:10, far from meaning to immerse, a word closely related to *baptizo* actually means to sprinkle. The writer of Hebrews speaks about 'various ceremonial washings' and uses the Greek word *baptismos* to describe them. In the rest of Hebrews 9 the writer spells out what these 'various ceremonial washings' are. Hebrews 9:13 refers to Numbers 19:17-18; Hebrews 9:19 to Exodus 24:6-8; and Hebrews 9:21 to Leviticus 8:19 and 16:14. These 'various ceremonial washings' included the ceremony of the red heifer, the Day of Atonement, and Moses sprinkling the scroll and the people. The significant feature about all these was that the mode employed was sprinkling, not immersion. So the New Testament, in at least one place, actually links *baptizo* with sprinkling.

It is difficult to see how baptists can prove from Scripture the first element in their classic argument for immersion, namely, that *bapto* and *baptizo* always mean to immerse. 'The assertion that the command to baptize is a command to immerse [is] utterly unauthorised [by Scripture] and unreasonable.'[8] Greek has two verbs, which mean to immerse and nothing but to immerse, but they are not the verbs *baptizo* and *bapto*.

In fact, these two Greek verbs, which mean to

immerse and nothing but to immerse, are never used of baptism in the New Testament.

2. The New Testament's description of some baptisms implies immersion.

In their accounts of Jesus' baptism, both Matthew and Mark write about Jesus coming up out of the water. Baptists claim that this implies he went down under the water and came up from under the water (Matthew 3:16; Mark 1:10). This claim rests on the Greek prepositions used by Matthew and Mark. Mark uses the preposition *ek*, while Matthew uses the preposition *apo*. While *ek* does mean 'out of', *apo* does not mean 'out of' but only 'away from'. Both writers are clearly describing the same event, so Mark is using *ek* in the sense of *apo*. What Matthew and Mark are saying is that Jesus went away from the waters of the River Jordan, and not that he came up from under the waters. '[Neither] of the Greek prepositions ... ever carry the meaning of down into or up ... from under. This is certainly reading far too much into *ek* [and] *apo*.'[9]

Baptists also claim that the baptism of the Ethiopian Eunuch by Philip implies immersion (Acts 8:38-39). Again it is said that the idea of immersion is found in Luke's use of the phrases 'went down into the water' and 'came up out of the water'. However, because similar expressions are used of the Ethiopian Eunuch's baptism as are used of Jesus' baptism, it is reasonable to assume that they mean the same thing. The movement is simply to and from the water, not beneath the surface of the water to above it.

This interpretation is underlined by the fact that Luke says that both Philip and the Ethiopian eunuch were involved in the going down into the water and the coming up out of it, a point highlighted in the Authorised Version. It says, 'they went down both into the water, both Philip and the eunuch.' If this movement implies immersion, then Philip immersed himself as well as the eunuch, and that seems unlikely. What happened was probably this: after the chariot stopped, both Philip and the eunuch walked to the water and entered it. Then Philip baptised the eunuch. This done, they both came up from the water, at which point Philip was suddenly taken away by the Holy Spirit. The mode of the eunuch's baptism is not at all said to be immersion.

So, once again it is difficult to understand how baptists can prove from Scripture the second element in their classic argument for immersion, namely, that the New Testament's description of certain baptisms implies immersion.

3. The meaning of baptism is symbolised only by immersion.

Baptists claim that, since baptism represents union with Christ in his death and resurrection, immersion in water and emergence from it is the best expression of this. They point to Romans 6:3-4 and Colossians 2:12 as evidence for their assertion. However, a careful analysis of Romans 6:3-6 will show that there is no necessary allusion to the mode of baptism.

In this passage Paul is dealing with the believer's union with Christ, something signified by baptism. He describes that union, at the start of Romans 6:4, as being 'buried with him'. What baptists do is to take hold of this expression and insist that only immersion provides a picture of burial. However, they fail to take into account the fact that Paul describes the believer's union with Christ, not just in terms of being buried together, but also, in Romans 6:5, in terms of being planted together and, in Romans 6:6, in terms of being crucified together. These last two expressions indicate union with Christ as much as being buried with him, but they do not bear any analogy to immersion. John Murray has highlighted the weakness of the baptist claim that Romans 6:3-6 points to immersion:

> It is very easy to focus attention upon one or two of the terms which Paul here uses and make it appear that the indispensable mode of baptism is after the analogy of what we have arbitrary selected. ... We are represented as having hung on the cross together with Christ, and that phase of union with Christ is represented by our baptism into Christ not one whit less than our death in him and our burial with him, not one whit less than our being planted with him in the likeness of his death and our being raised with him in the power of his resurrection. When all of Paul's expressions are taken into account we see that burial with Christ can be appealed to as providing an index to the mode of baptism no more than can crucifixion with him. And since the latter does not indicate the mode of baptism there is no validity to the argument that burial does. The fact is that there are many aspects to our union with Christ. It is arbitrary to select one aspect and find in the language used to set it forth the essence of the mode of baptism. Such procedure is indefensible unless it can be carried through

consistently. It cannot be carried through
consistently here and therefore it is arbitrary and
invalid.[10]

This idea that the meaning of baptism is symbolised
only by immersion can be rejected on more practical
grounds. The only other record in the New Testament
of someone being both buried and raised to life is that
of Lazarus in John 11:38-44. Because Jesus was buried
and, by implication, raised to life in the same way as
Lazarus, this casts doubts on the baptist assertion that
immersion is the mode of baptism.

Baptists claim that going down under the water
represents Jesus going down into the grave. But there is
no proof whatever that Christ's burial was a going
down into a hole dug in the ground. On the contrary, '...
his grave was a cave cut out of the side of a rock, like
that of Lazarus. ... To say that in "going down into the
water" he is burying his body just as his master's body
was buried in the grave is to say what cannot be
proved'.[11]

Baptists also claim that coming up from under the
water represents Jesus being raised up from the dead.
However, 'burial (and, by implication, resurrection)
would not normally be thought of ... in terms of an
immersion movement i.e., down and up'.[12] Jesus did
not command Lazarus to *come up* from his grave, but to
come out from his tomb. John records that Lazarus did
not come up but came out. If Jesus' body, like Lazarus'
corpse, was laid on a shelf in his tomb, horizontal to or
even above the ground, then the movement in Jesus'
resurrection was not a down and up one. So, once more
it is hard to see how the baptists can prove from

Scripture the third element in their classic argument for immersion, namely, that the significance of baptism is expressed only by immersion.

In the Scottish legal system, three verdicts can be given: guilty, not guilty, and not proven. The case for baptism by immersion is, at best, not proven. When the three pillars upon which it rests are examined in the light of God's Word, they are found to be insecure indeed.

Contrary to what is frequently assumed, the case for pouring or sprinkling as the proper mode of baptism has strong biblical support.

1. Throughout the Bible there is a clear connection between sprinkling and the salvation offered in the Covenant of Grace.

A few examples of this connection may be noted.

Exodus 24 records how God's covenant with Israel at Mount Sinai was ratified through the sprinkling of blood:

Then [Moses] sent young Israelite men, and they offered burnt offerings and sacrificed young bulls as fellowship offerings to the LORD. Moses took half of the blood and put it in bowls and the other half he sprinkled on the altar. Then he took the Book of the Covenant and read it to the people. They responded, 'We will do everything the LORD has said. We will obey.' Moses then took the blood, sprinkled it on the people and said, 'This is the blood of the covenant that the LORD has made with you in accordance with all these words.'

The way that the covenant was ratified through the sprinkling of blood pointed forward to how Jesus would ratify the new administration of the covenant of grace (which is called 'the new covenant') by the sprinkling of his blood. The writer of the book of Hebrews says as much in Hebrews 12:24. So the mode associated with the ratification of the covenant of grace was sprinkling, the sprinkling of the blood of Jesus the mediator.

In Ezekiel 36:25-28 there is a very comprehensive description of the salvation God offers under the terms of the covenant of grace. God promises cleansing from sin, regeneration and the gift of the Holy Spirit leading to sanctification.

'I will cleanse you from all your impurities. ... I will give you a new heart and put a new spirit in you. I will remove from you your heart of stone and give you a heart of flesh. And I will put my Spirit in you and move you to follow my decrees. ... You will be my people and I will be your God.'

This passage also speaks about a mode which will signify this salvation. It is not immersion, but sprinkling: 'I will sprinkle clean water on you.' There is no mention of immersion; only sprinkling.

Most people will agree that, in Isaiah 52:13-53:12, there is the most wonderful description of Jesus' work on the cross. All the blessings that Jesus, the mediator of the covenant, will secure by his substitutionary death just saturate this passage. Right at the start of these verses, Isaiah gives a summary description of Jesus' work, using a term that gathers together everything that Jesus will achieve by his death on the cross: 'So will he sprinkle many nations' (Isaiah 52:15).

The New Testament writers pick up on this Old Testament connection between sprinkling and the salvation offered in the covenant of grace. In Hebrews 10:22, the writer says that Christians are those who have had their 'hearts sprinkled to cleanse [them] from a guilty conscience'. In 1 Peter 1:2, Peter describes Christians, those who have experienced God's salvation, as those 'who have been chosen ... for ... sprinkling by [Jesus'] blood'.

There is a strong connection between sprinkling and the salvation offered in the covenant of grace. Paedobaptists argue that because there is this connection and because baptism is a sign of the salvation offered in the covenant of grace, then the preferable mode of baptism is sprinkling.

2. The mode of baptism must correspond to the meaning of baptism.

Baptists are correct in making something of the mode of baptism because it cannot be separated from the meaning of baptism. The meaning of a sacrament is either disclosed or obscured by the mode of observing the sacrament. 'Correct meaning can be communicated only by the correct mode.'[13]

But what does baptism signify? It points to God's salvation in Jesus coming to us as the Spirit falls upon us to bring cleansing from sin and union with Jesus. The best mode to represent this is pouring or sprinkling as water falls on us from above.

3. The first Christians baptised by sprinkling or pouring.

The general idea of baptism was not something new that had been introduced by Jesus, or the apostles, or even John the Baptist. It was a common practice among the Jews. Even before they became followers of Jesus, the first Christians, who were Jewish, were familiar with the general idea of baptism from the rituals of Judaism. These baptisms were carried out by pouring or sprinkling. Surely it is reasonable to assume that, when they began practising baptism themselves, the first Christians would have used a mode they were already familiar with, namely, pouring or sprinkling.

Another indicator that the first Christians baptised by pouring or sprinkling is the fact that the early church had its roots firmly planted in the Old Testament. For example, worship services were based on the worship services in the synagogue, and the Lord's Supper on the Passover.

Central to their understanding of baptism was the idea of cleansing from sin. On three occasions the Old Testament links cleansing with bathing, and this could possibly hint at immersion: Leviticus 14:8; 15:13; Numbers 19:19. However, in the majority of occasions, it links cleansing with sprinkling: Leviticus 14:7; 16:19; Numbers 19:13, 20, 21; Ezekiel 36:25. It would seem perfectly natural to assume that, when they were administering a sacrament which symbolised cleansing, the first Christians would fall back on their Old Testament heritage and use the same mode associated with cleansing in the Old Testament, namely, sprinkling.

Further, if the first Christians were going to make

such a radical break from their Old Testament roots and immerse instead of pouring or sprinkling, it is very likely that the New Testament writers would have mentioned this radical break. That they do not signal any such break seems to imply that no radical break took place, and the early church employed the mode of baptism used in the Old Testament, namely, pouring or sprinkling.

Although it is evidence from outside the Bible, *the Didache*, an early second-century document which gives 'an accurate and contemporary picture of the early church community',[14] says it was the early church's practice to 'pour forth water thrice upon the head'[15] when administering baptism.

4. The mass baptism on the Day of Pentecost.

The mass baptism that took place on the Day of Pentecost is a further indicator that the first Christians baptised by pouring or sprinkling. It is certainly possible that the apostles could have baptised the three thousand converts by immersion. However, there are practical problems with this theory. 'Twelve men seeking to lower and raise three thousand converts in and out of ... water would fall from exhaustion before they could finish.'[16] Even if Peter and the Eleven enlisted the help of others, it is highly unlikely that the Jewish authorities, who only a short time previously had killed Jesus, would give his followers permission to use Jerusalem's pools for mass baptisms. It would be very doubtful if the enemies of the Lord Jesus Christ who seven weeks before had planted his cross on Calvary ... [would] put the city water pools at [the apostles'] disposal for the administration of the

distinctive rite of this hated sect.[17] To do so would have
been an 'extraordinary courtesy'.[18]

What could have happened is that the three
thousand were baptised by sprinkling *en masse*.

> Towards the end of the inter-testamental period, ...
> [Pentecost] began ... to be observed as the
> anniversary of the giving of the law at Mount Sinai,
> because this was reckoned as having happened fifty
> days after the Exodus.[19]

At Sinai Moses sprinkled blood *en masse* on the whole
nation of Israel. On the Day of Pentecost Peter could
have followed Moses' precedent and baptised the three
thousand *en masse* by sprinkling. However, what is
more likely to have happened is that Peter, assisted by
the Eleven, baptised the three thousand converts by
pouring water on them.

> Allowing for an average of only one baptism per
> minute, twelve baptizers could accomplish [the
> baptism of] three thousand converts in less than five
> hours ... far away from the prying eyes of the
> enemies of those ... who were professing faith in
> Christ.[20]

5. John's baptism

There can be no disputing the fact that John baptised. It
was this that earned him the title 'the Baptist'. What
mode did John use as he baptised? Baptists would
claim that, because the verb *baptizo* is used in
connection with John's baptising activity, he baptised
by immersion. Their claim is based on the premise that

baptizo can only mean to immerse. However, in the light of the fact that *baptizo* does not necessarily indicate immersion, an understanding of the mode of baptism John used has to be gained from other considerations.

A case can be made out that John actually baptised by pouring or sprinkling. Consider *the origin of John's baptism*. It seems incorrect to look for the origin of John's baptism outside the Old Testament in view of the fact that the rest of John's thought and behaviour is rooted in the Old Testament. The origin of John's baptism is to be found in the ritual washings of the Old Testament, and these were carried out by pouring or sprinkling, and not by immersion.

Consider *the meaning of John's baptism*. Luke 3:16 indicates that it was meant, in part, to be a prophetic sign, pointing forward to a future cleansing from sin that would be achieved on the basis of the activity of Jesus, the more powerful one who would come after John. As we noted earlier, there is a connection between cleansing from sin and sprinkling. John, whose thinking had its roots in the Old Testament, would have been aware of this connection. So, if John wanted his baptism to point to a future cleansing from sin, it would have been unlikely that he would bypass sprinkling, a mode with strong links with cleansing from sin in the Old Testament, in favour of immersion, a mode with no clear links with cleansing from sin.

Consider *the investigation into John's baptism*, which is recorded in John 1:19-20. Based on Old Testament passages such as Isaiah 52:15 and Ezekiel 36:25 which describe the Messiah's work in terms of sprinkling, there was an expectation among the Jews that the Messiah would identify himself by sprinkling. In the minds of those sent to investigate John's baptism there was such a strong connection between the Messiah and sprinkling that, when they saw John baptising, they asked him if he was the Messiah. There would have been no reason for them to ask that question had John not been baptising in a way associated with the anticipated Messiah, namely, sprinkling.

Consider *the fulfilment of John's baptism*. In Matthew 3:11, Mark 1:8, Luke 3:16 and John 1:33, John predicted that his baptism with water pointed forward to a baptism of the Holy Sprit to be carried out by Jesus. John's prophecy was fulfilled on the Day of Pentecost. The baptism by the Spirit cannot be conceived of as an immersion. In Acts 2:17, it is specifically described as a pouring out. If the baptism by the Spirit was by pouring, then John's baptism, which anticipated it, would also appropriately be administered by pouring. 'Shall the type be after a totally different mode?'[21] asks Charles Hodge, and obviously expects a negative answer.

In the light of these four considerations, it appears that the mode of baptism employed by John the Baptist was not immersion, but pouring or sprinkling.

6. Jesus' baptism

Jesus' baptism is of supreme importance for us. The mode of his baptism should be the mode we use. It can be argued that he was baptised by pouring or sprinkling. In support of this, we may point to the fact that Jesus was baptised by John, and (as I have previously suggested) he baptised by pouring or sprinkling.

We can also point to the meaning of Jesus' baptism. In Luke 4:21, at the conclusion of his sermon in the synagogue at Nazareth, Jesus claimed that he was the Messiah as he applied the prophecy of Isaiah 61:1-2 to himself. The reason he did so was, as the start of Luke 4:18 indicates, because the Lord had anointed him. When did this anointing take place? At his baptism which was his anointing with the Spirit for his Messianic work as prophet, priest and king. John Calvin describes Jesus' baptism as 'the visible symbol of [his] sacred anointing'.[22] If this is so, it is improbable that Jesus was immersed in the Jordan because immersion cannot depict anointing. 'How can an "anointing", a "coming down upon", or a "resting upon" be symbolised by immersion?'[23] Pouring or sprinkling is the mode which best symbolises Jesus' anointing with the Holy Spirit at his baptism.

If Jesus' baptism was his anointing as the Messiah, then, as well as being his anointing to be a prophet and king, it was also his ordination to the priesthood. There is an indication in Matthew 21, Mark 11 and Luke 20 that this was one of the ways in which Jesus viewed his baptism. Matthew 21:12-16, Mark 11:15-17 and Luke 19:45-47 record how Jesus, acting in a priestly capacity, cleansed the temple. Commenting on the incident, Calvin says, 'there is no doubt of the fact that he is testifying to himself as ... High Priest, who presides over the temple.'[24] The next day the Jewish religious authorities challenged Jesus about his action: 'Tell us by what authority you are doing these things? Who gave you this authority?' (Luke 20:2). These questions do not relate to his ministry in general but to Jesus' specific priestly action of cleansing the temple.

In Luke 20:4, Jesus immediately defended his right to act in this priestly capacity by asking a question about John's baptism which he had experienced. 'John's baptism – was it from heaven, or from men?' When politicians are being interviewed on the television and are asked an awkward question, they often try to get out of a potentially embarrassing situation by asking a question themselves. Some people have thought that Jesus was doing that sort of thing here. However, Jesus was not just using a debating technique to avoiding having to answer an awkward question.

His answer was 'not a red herring to lead them away from their questions'.[25] His reply had a direct bearing on the question of his authority. Jesus was linking his priestly activity in cleansing the temple with his baptism by John. He was claiming that it was his baptism by John which gave him the authority to act in this priestly manner, and he was able to reason this way because he saw his baptism as his ordination to the priesthood. Jesus was saying he had every right to act as a priest and purify the temple from defilement because he had been ordained to the priesthood when John baptised him.

How was a priest ordained? According to Numbers 4:3 and 47, he had to be thirty years old, which Jesus was when he was baptised (Luke 3:23). Then, according to Exodus 28:1, a priest had to be called by God as Aaron the first High Priest was, and Jesus was called (Hebrews 5:4-10).

Also, according to Exodus 29:9 and Numbers 25:13, a priest had to be ordained by someone who already was a priest. Jesus' baptism was performed by John, who, as well as undoubtedly being a prophet,

also had the priestly credentials to carry out an
ordination to the priesthood. He came from a priestly
family. Also central to his ministry was the way he
baptised others, and his baptism had its origins in and
was administered according to the priestly rituals of the
Old Testament. One writer argues that John should be
known as 'John the Purifier',[26] and purification was a
priestly activity. John appears to stand in both the
priestly and prophetic traditions, and so was qualified
to carry out a valid ordination to the priesthood.

Most significant of all, according to Numbers 8:6-
7, in order to be ordained, a priest must be sprinkled
with water. In the light of the way Jesus viewed his
baptism as his ordination to the priesthood, it appears
that this Old Testament regulation was fulfilled when
John sprinkled Jesus with water rather than immersing
him in it.

Jay Adams is correct when he writes, 'if [the Bible
teaches] pouring, we ought to pour; if immersion, we
ought to immerse.'[27] The weight of evidence seems to
point away from immersion towards pouring or
sprinkling as the preferable mode of baptism. Having
said that, we must not reject baptism by immersion as
invalid. The validity of baptism does not depend on the
quantity of water employed or the mode used. So,
although we believe that pouring or sprinkling is the
preferable mode of baptism, we accept immersion as
legitimate because water is administered in the name of
the Triune God by a lawfully ordained minister.

Nor do we value the Christian fellowship of baptists
any less because they were baptised by immersion!
The basis of Christian fellowship is not a particular
understanding of the mode of baptism. It is that our

great and covenant God sent his one and only Son to
shed his blood for us and, by the gracious activity of his
Holy Spirit in our lives, brought us to faith in Jesus and
adopted us into his family, so that we are now brothers
and sisters in Christ. May we never be guilty of
substituting anything for that! Christians may disagree
with each other over many things connected with
baptism, yet still love each other and value mutual
fellowship because they are in Christ. Let us hold our
views about baptism firmly and with conviction, but
also in love and with understanding towards those who
differ from us, never allowing different views on
baptism to become barriers to fellowship between
God's people.

References
1. Uprichard, 5.
2. Strong, 933.
3. *Westminster Confession of Faith*, Chapter 28, Section
III.
4. C. G. Kirkby, *Signs and Seals of the Covenant* (Belfast,
Northern Ireland: Privately printed, n.d.), 115.
5. *Westminster Confession of Faith*, Chapter 28, Section
III.
6. Strong, 938.
7. Alexander Carson, *Baptism in its Modes and Subjects*
(Philadelphia, 1845), 19.
8. Charles Hodge, *Systematic Theology vol. 3* (Grand
Rapids, Michigan: William B. Eerdmans Publishing
Company, 1946), 526-527.
9. Jay E. Adams, *The Meaning and Mode of Baptism*
(Nutley, New Jersey: Presbyterian and Reformed
Publishing Company, 1976), 41-42.
10. John Murray, *Christian Baptism* (Nutley, New Jersey:

Presbyterian and Reformed Publishing Company, 1977), 30-31.

11. J. C. Ryle, *Knots Untied* (London: James Clarke and Company Limited, 1954), 70.

12. Uprichard, 31.

13. Adams, vi-vii.

14. E. C. Whitaker, *Documents of the Baptismal Liturgy* (London: SPCK, 1960), 1.

15. *Ibid.*, 1.

16. Duane Edward Spencer, *Holy Baptism : Word Keys which Unlock the Covenant* (Tyler, Texas: Geneva Ministries, 1984), 108.

17. James W. Dale, *An Inquiry into the Usage of Baptizo and the Nature of Christic and Patristic Baptism* (Philadelphia: W. Rudder Company, 1874), 155-156.

18. *Ibid.*, 156.

19. John R. W. Stott, *The Message of Acts* (Leicester, England: Inter-Varsity Press, 1990), 62.

20. Spencer, 108.

21. Hodge, *The Mode and Subjects of Baptism* (Belfast, Northern Ireland: Privately printed, n.d.), 12.

22. John Calvin, *Institutes of Christian Religion*, II.xv.5.

23. Adams, 20.

24. John Calvin, *A Harmony of the Gospels Matthew, Mark and Luke. Volume 3*. Trans. by A. W. Morrison (Edinburgh, Scotland: The Saint Andrew Press, 1972), 3.

25. Leon Morris, *The Gospel According to Matthew* (Leicester, England: Inter-Varsity Press, 1992), 534.

26. James W. Dale, *Johannic Baptism* (Phillipsburg, New Jersey: Presbyterian and Reformed Publishing Company, 1993, reprint; Philadelphia: Presbyterian Board of Publication and Sabbath-School Work, 1898), 410.

27. Adams, vi.

OTHER ISSUES CONNECTED
WITH BAPTISM

The importance of baptism.

Several years ago, I was chatting with some members of my congregation about their attitude to baptism. While most of them had a positive attitude to baptism, some were worried about the controversy it can generate. 'How important is baptism anyway?' one understandably asked.

Two dangers need to be avoided. On the one hand, there is the danger of *overvaluing* the importance of baptism. This is the mistake the Roman Catholic Church makes when it insists that a person cannot be saved without it: 'God has bound salvation to the sacrament of Baptism.'[1]

On the other hand, there is the danger of *undervaluing* the importance of baptism. This is the position taken by those who argue that, (1) if the sign and seal of baptism is outward and not necessarily inward, so that not all who are baptised are saved, and, (2) since the Holy Spirit is sovereign, working how he pleases, so that he not only can but may regenerate people without the sacraments as he sometimes does without the Word – then baptism is not all that important.

The way to avoid these two dangers is to walk a middle path that stresses the importance but not the absolute necessity of baptism. This middle path is summarised in the *Westminster Confession of Faith*, which teaches that, while baptism is so important that 'it is a great sin to condemn or neglect this sacrament'[2], it is not indispensable to salvation so 'one can be saved ... without baptism, and ... not everyone who is baptised is ... reborn'.[3]

Baptism is important. Jesus commanded it and nothing that Jesus instituted should be undervalued. Furthermore, baptism is a way God uses to strengthen the believer's faith. Baptism does not create faith.

The Roman Catholic Church is wrong when it teaches that 'the baptismal water is the instrument Christ uses to effect redemptive purification'.[4] Baptism does not transmit grace simply by being administered. John Murray rightly expresses the Bible's position when he writes:

> The sign and seal does not bring into existence that which is signified or sealed. It does not effect union with Christ. ... Baptism does not convey or confer the grace which it signifies. Baptism is a means of grace but not a means of conferring the grace represented.[5]

Baptism strengthens the faith that is already in existence, so those who undervalue baptism end up spiritually impoverished.

How does baptism act as a means of grace? Baptism strengthens the believer's faith as he looks back to his baptism, remembers what it signifies, and recalls how God has been true to his promises and brought him to faith in Jesus. Calvin is helpful. In Calvin's *Catechism* the question is asked: 'When is it that the sacraments have their effect?' and the reply given is this: 'When a man receives them in faith, seeking only in them Christ and his grace.'[6]

This reception by faith of the benefits of baptism is not bound to a single moment. It depends on the spiritual condition of the believer on each occasion he recalls his baptism. Each time he remembers his baptism is like a new reception by faith of the benefits of his baptism, and the stronger the believer's faith, the more he gains from recalling his baptism. Being spiritually strengthened by baptism is something that goes on throughout the Christian's life.

> When our God and Father promised to save man by the blood of Jesus Christ and to renew him by the Holy Spirit He established baptism to be not only a sign, but also the ... pledge of these remarkable promises. Today no Christian, if he has been well instructed in the things of God, can recall his own baptism ... without experiencing a strengthening of his faith, ... and without being confirmed in the assurance that he is indeed the adopted son of God, the brother of Jesus Christ, and a member of the covenant of grace. ... The Christian, by his faith, ought to render the blessings which are and remain signified and offered by his baptism, an ever-present reality in his daily life. He ought constantly to refer back ... without ceasing to his baptism in order to gather progressively from it its fruit, in accordance with his faith.[7]

The status of the baptised child.

Among paedobaptists, there are three commonly held views about the status of the baptised child:

(1) all baptised children are elect and regenerated at some time or another;

(2) should they die before the age of accountability, all baptised children are thereby shown to be and to have been regenerated;

(3) all baptised children are not necessarily elect, but some are, and there is a great hope and even probability that baptised children reared faithfully in the nurture and admonition of the Lord will be brought to the Lord savingly.[8]

However, whatever view is adopted, the baptised infant will not come to faith in Jesus – something that his baptism summons him to – automatically. His parents must play their part. God uses means, and the means he uses in the spiritual development of baptised infants are the prayers, teaching and example of the child's parents. No-one has expressed this better than John Murray:

> Covenant privilege always entails covenant responsibility.... The Scripture does not extend to parents who have received baptism for their children... an assurance or guarantee that the children concerned are without condition the partakers of the grace signified and sealed by baptism.... God's covenant grace to children... always has an environment. The environment is, in a word, faithfulness.... The degree of ... assurance that God's promise to them will be fulfilled is proportionate to the extent ... of the keeping of his

covenant.... Such faithfulness to God's covenant ...
includes all that is involved in the bringing up of
children in the nurture and admonition of the
Lord.... This nurture is the means through which
God's covenant grace and promise come to
realisation and fruition.[9]

The question of rebaptism.

One Sunday afternoon many years ago my customary
Sunday afternoon rest was shattered by the sound of
the telephone. It was a member of the Youth
Fellowship. 'Sorry, I'll not be out at church tonight.
One of my mates is being baptised in the Pentecostal
church, and he has asked me along.' 'Who is it?' I
asked. When I was told the name, I was a little
surprised because I knew him to be a youth leader in a
neighbouring Presbyterian church. Since that Sunday
afternoon, I have been confronted with the issue of
rebaptism on many occasions.

Let me immediately point out that the term
'rebaptism' is misleading. Baptism can be administered 'only once to a person'.[10] Baptism is a sign of our
union with Christ, our regeneration, our forgiveness of
sins, and our receiving the Holy Spirit. These are
aspects of our salvation that happen only once. So 'the
reason why the sign of baptism is given only once is the
decisive, once-for-all character'[11] of what it signifies.
A rebaptism cannot be done because, once a person is
baptised, he cannot be unbaptised. The issue at the
centre of the question of rebaptism is the validity of the
person's baptism.

Why do people want to be 'rebaptised'? Some
deem their baptism invalid because it was carried out

by sprinkling while they were infants. Those who object to their baptism on these grounds usually hold that immersion as an adult believer is the only valid form of baptism. 'I wanted to be baptised properly' was the answer I received from a student who told me she had been rebaptised. Such people need to be given clear instruction on what the Bible teaches about baptism being a sign of God's grace, and not a sign of faith, about the baptism of believers' children as being a proper baptism, and about baptism being correctly administered by pouring or sprinkling.

Others argue that their baptism was invalid because their parents, who presented them for baptism, were not Christians. If neither of the parents were believers, baptism should never take place. However, the primary emphasis in baptism is on God's grace, which is proclaimed and offered in the sacrament. God's promise, which is sealed in baptism, is stronger than human sin. This suggests that there is another way to view their experience: their conversion is the fulfilment of baptism. To profess our faith as an adult, even if our parents were not believers, is to confirm our baptism and the promises of God's grace it portrays.

Some regard their baptism as invalid because it took place in a heretical church. If a baptism took place in a church that denies the biblical teaching about the Trinity, such as a Unitarian church, then it must be regarded as an invalid baptism. A legitimate baptism is one in which a lawfully called gospel minister administers water in the name of the triune God. A church which denies the doctrine of the Trinity cannot perform a valid baptism.

Some have objected to the use of a trinitarian

formula in the administration of baptism because, elsewhere in the New Testament, baptism is 'in the name of Jesus Christ' or 'into the name of Jesus Christ', without any mention of a trinitarian formula.[12] However, in response to this objection, it should be noted that:

> Christ's command to baptize would inevitably carry a reference back to his own baptism, when the Father was heard addressing him as the Son, and the Spirit descended to seal him as the Son sent by the Father. Baptism into Christ, or in his name, involves the coming of the Spirit from the Father in the name of the Son.[13]

What about a baptism that has taken place within the Roman Catholic Church? Do converted Roman Catholics need to be rebaptised? Is their Roman Catholic baptism invalid? Some argue that converted Roman Catholics should be rebaptised to show that they have broken free of Roman Catholicism and as an act of distancing themselves from their former beliefs. Others argue that converted Roman Catholics should be rebaptised because the Roman Catholic understanding of baptism is completely different from the biblical understanding of baptism.

Historically, the Reformation churches regarded the rebaptism of converted Roman Catholics as unnecessary. Even Roman Catholic baptism fulfils the criterion for a valid baptism as set out in the *Westminster Confession of Faith*. Calvin insisted that although he and others had been baptised 'in the Papacy by wicked men and idolaters', their baptism was still valid because 'by baptism we were initiated, not into the name of any man, but into the Name of the Father, Son and Holy Spirit, and therefore that baptism is not of man, but of God, by whomsoever it may be administered'.[14] Hodge underlines this when he writes:

> Romanish baptism fulfils all the conditions of valid baptism as given in our Standards. It is a washing with water in the Name of the Trinity, with the ostensible and professed design of making the recipient a member of the visible church, and a partaker in its benefits.[15]

No matter how sincere the reasons for wanting it, the idea of rebaptism is misguided. Instead of rebaptism, what we need to do is to remember what baptism signifies, and this is something that we should do daily throughout the whole of our Christian lives. As, by faith, we remember what God has promised to us in our baptism, at that moment, we receive what God has promised.

> In remembering baptism, we are entering (a little more each time) into what God has done in and for us in this sacrament, calling into the present the power of what ... happened in the past, deepening our understanding of what we could never fully understand at the time of our baptism as infants, ... and appropriating more and more the grace made available to us.[16]

Baptism is something that Christians should be constantly seeking to remember but never wanting to repeat.

Non-Christian parents
The major area of difficulty in the practical administration of baptism is the situation which arises with increasing frequency. Some parents want their child baptised but genuinely feel unable to profess that they are Christians. 'There is no way that we will tell lies and say that we are Christians,' one couple said. 'Yet we want our baby baptised.' What action can be taken in a situation like that?

Sponsors
One course of action suggested is that the child should be baptised but with sponsors taking the vows on behalf of the parents. But this idea of sponsors is foreign to biblical teaching. We base our understanding of baptism on the doctrine of the covenant of grace. Children are baptised because God is not only our God, but the God and Father of our children. If this is the reason for administering baptism to children, then it hardly makes sense to have baptismal sponsors present children for baptism.

A service of thanksgiving
A more common course of action is to offer a service of thanksgiving for the child, in which no vows are taken and no water administered. Those who offer a service of thanksgiving defend their practice on several grounds. They believe that parents should be rewarded and not penalised for their honesty. They have counselled parents for baptism, who were honest enough to say that they are not Christians, even though they knew that meant their child would not be baptised. However, they have also counselled other parents,

who, in their opinion, were not Christians, but were, again in their opinion, prepared to lie and say they were in order to get their child baptised. They feel that not offering a service of thanksgiving was penalising them for being honest.

Some offer services of thanksgiving on purely pragmatic grounds. They claim that, if they offer no alternative to baptism, they will turn people away from the church and they will be lost to the gospel. They maintain that services of thanksgiving create openings in otherwise closed homes. If these parents see that the church is not rejecting them, it is said, they might start coming to church or sending their children to Sunday School and the congregation's youth organisations. Some proponents of services of thanksgiving offer a more theological justification for their practice. They argue from common grace. God in his goodness gives good gifts to all people, including the gift of children. So everyone should be able to thank him for these gifts, and a service of thanksgiving provides such an opportunity.

In spite of the attempts of those who carry out services of thanksgiving to justify their practice, they are trying to defend the indefensible. Fundamentally, this specific type of service of thanksgiving, *as an alternative to baptism*, is not taught in the Bible.

'God is not to be worshipped ... in any other way than that prescribed in Holy Scripture'[17] is the principle upon which worship is to be based. To import into worship something not taught in the Bible, such as this type of service of thanksgiving, is spiritually dangerous and dishonours God. In addition, the claim that non-Christian parents should be given the opportunity to thank God for the gift of their child also dishonours God. How can parents, who are covenant breakers because they are not believers, stand before the covenant God and thank him for the gift of their child, when, by their lives and actions, they are constantly rejecting God's greatest gift, namely, Jesus? Looking at the service of thanksgiving in this way turns it into an act of hypocrisy.

Another objection to this type of service of thanksgiving is that God and his grace are not glorified in them. In a service of thanksgiving, the emphasis is on what the parents do. They are giving thanks to God. In a baptism, the emphasis is on something completely different. It is on what God does. In a service of thanksgiving, the parents take centre stage, but, in a baptism, God takes centre stage. From a practical point of view, this type of service of thanksgiving creates confusion in people's minds. No matter how carefully it is explained that a service of thanksgiving for a child is not the same as baptism, people still regard it as a baptism, albeit no water is involved. My own view is that any other form of service which may, in any way, be associated with baptism but is not really baptism dishonours Jesus, who instituted the sacrament.

Refusal

A third course of action is to refuse baptism. This is something that should be done only after a long period of instruction and reflection for the parents. The conditions for baptism should be clearly and faithfully set out, and then the parents requesting baptism assisted to examine themselves to see if they can fulfil the biblical conditions. When this is done sensitively and prayerfully, the non-Christian parents may well realise themselves that they are not Christians and withdraw their request for baptism.

An evangelistic opportunity

Very often, with the arrival of a new child into the home, non-Christian parents are more open to spiritual things than normal. The responsibility of bringing children into the world and raising them weighs heavily upon them. They want to do the best for their child, and this gives the opportunity to tell them that the best thing they could do for their child is to trust in Jesus as their Saviour and Lord so that the child will be brought up in a truly Christian home. Requests for baptism present evangelistic opportunities, since people may be willing to listen to the gospel more readily than usual.

The couple I mentioned earlier on, who said, 'There is no way that we will tell lies and say that we are Christians, yet we want our baby baptised', are one of the finest Christian couples in their congregation because their minister saw their request for baptism as an evangelistic opportunity. We need to resist our natural inclination to refuse non-Christian couples request for baptism straightaway, and instead see it as a door that God has opened for us to reach them with the gospel.

References
1. *Catechism of the Catholic Church* (Dublin: Veritas, 1994), 285.
2. *Westminster Confession of Faith*, Chapter 28, Section V.

3. *Ibid.*, Chapter 28, Section V.

4. Burkhard Neunheuser, 'Baptism' In *Sacramentum Mundi* Vol. 1. (New York: Herder and Herder, 1968).

5. Murray, 86-87.

6. Horatius Bonar, ed., *Catechisms of the Scottish Reformation* (London: James Nisbet and Company, 1866), 75.

7. Marcel, 170, 172.

8. *Ibid.*, 143.

9. John Murray, 92.

10. *Westminster Confession of Faith*, Chapter 28, Section VII.

11. Hendry, 228.

12. Acts 2:38; Acts 8:16; Acts 10:48; Acts 19:5.

13. T. F. Torrance, *The Biblical Doctrine of Baptism* (Edinburgh, Scotland: The Saint Andrew Press, 1958), 21.

14. John Calvin, *Institutes of the Christian Religion*, 20.

15. Charles Hodge, *The Church and its Polity* (London: Thomas Nelson and Sons), 199.

16. Quoted in Michael Green, *Baptism: Its Purpose, Practice and Power* (London: Hodder and Stoughton, 1987), 125.

17. *Westminster Confession of Faith*, Chapter 21, Section I.

AN ANNOTATED BIBLIOGRAPHY

Jay E. Adams, *The Meaning and Mode of Baptism*, Nutley, New Jersey: Presbyterian and Reformed Publishing Company, 1976. In his usual easily understood way, Adams establishes that the proper mode of baptism is not immersion but pouring / sprinkling. He stresses that the mode of baptism cannot be separated from the meaning of baptism, because the correct meaning can only be conveyed by the correct mode. He shows that mode which communicates aright the meaning of baptism is pouring / sprinkling.

Robert R. Booth, *Children of Promise: The Biblical Case for Infant Baptism*, Philipsburg, New Jersey: Presbyterian and Reformed Publishing Company, 1996. This book was written to explain why the author moved from a baptist position of baptism to a paedobaptist one. He first explains what paedobaptism is not and then what he believes the Bible requires of Christian parents. Booth presents his case in a gentle, yet clear and convincing manner.

John Calvin, *Institutes of the Christian Religion*, Edited by John T. McNeill, Translated by Ford Lewis Battles, Philadelphia: The Westminster Press, 1960. Although Calvin's treatment of baptism in general and infant baptism in particular in Book 4 Chapters 15 and 16 may not be exhaustive, it is seminal. Later paedobaptist writers of any note stand on Calvin's shoulders, developing his ideas more fully.

Michael Green, *Baptism*, London: Hodder and Stoughton, 1987. Any young Christian, who wanted to think through the issues involved in the whole question of baptism, would find this book helpful, especially his treatment of the objections to infant baptism and the question of rebaptism.

Charles Hodge, *The Mode and Subjects of Baptism*, Belfast, Northern Ireland: Privately printed, 1966. No-one could fail to appreciate the paedobaptist position on the mode of baptism from the way Hodge thoroughly handles the topic.

C.G. Kirkby. *Signs and Seals of the Covenant: a Review of the Doctrine of Christian Baptism*. n.p., n.d. A well researched book. Its most interesting feature is that the author writes in support of infant baptism, yet he was originally a baptist.

Pierre Ch. Marcel, *The Biblical Doctrine of Infant Baptism*, Translated by Philip Edgcumbe Hughes, London: James Clarke and Company Limited, 1953. One of the best books on the paedobaptist understanding of baptism. What he says about baptism as a seal of the covenant and as a means of grace is outstanding.

John Murray, *Christian Baptism*, Nutley, New Jersey, Presbyterian and Reformed Publishing Company, 1980. Murray's book is a classic work on the biblical arguments for the paedobaptist understanding of baptism. His criticism of the baptist position and his analysis of the Bible's teaching about the meaning, mode, subjects and efficacy of baptism is thorough and meticulous. Anyone who is prepared to think will not fail to benefit from Murray's well-argued treatment of the issues.

John P. Sartelle, *Infant Baptism: what Christian parents should know*, Philipsburg, New Jersey: Presbyterian and Reformed Publishing Company, 1985. Sartelle sets out, in a concise way, the Bible's teaching about the baptism of covenant children. He is simple, but not simplistic, as he presents the basis and meaning of baptism. The usefulness of this book lies in the helpful way that Sartelle deals with questions which arise in thinking Christians' minds about baptism, and the practical instruction he gives about the Christian family and the responsibilities of parents towards their baptised children.

Duane Edward Spencer, *Holy Baptism: Word Keys which Unlock the Covenant*, Tyler, Texas: Geneva Ministries, 1984. This book deals exclusively with the mode of baptism. Although some might take exception to his combative and strongly polemical style, Spencer leaves no stone unturned as he demolishes the case for immersion, and as a consequence, the point of view that either immersion or pouring/sprinkling is an acceptable mode of baptism. He establishes conclusively from the Old and New Testament that the preferable mode for baptism is pouring / sprinkling.

R.E. H. Uprichard, *Baptism*, Belfast, Northern Ireland: Westminster Fellowship Trust, 1981. This short book outlines in an extremely helpful way the paedobaptist understanding of the meaning, subjects and mode of baptism.

Remember Jesus
A users guide to understanding
and enjoying Holy Communion

Steve Motyer

The other sacrament of the Christian church is the
Lord's Supper. Just as is the case with the sacrament
of baptism, the Lord's Supper is open to misunderstanding and confusion as well as to erroneous ideas
concerning its practice and benefits. Steve Motyer, a
lecturer in New Testament at London Bible College,
has written a useful book that gives a doctrinal
understanding of the significance of the Lord's Supper.
The book is in three sections. Section One deals with
several frequent questions that arise with regard to the
Lord's Supper. Section Two considers two important
passages of Scripture concerning the Lord's Supper:
(1) its original institution by Jesus Christ as recorded
in the Gospels; (2) the teaching of Paul given to the
church in Corinth. Section Three gives practical
guidelines for participating in this sacrament.

'Both new and mature Christians could read this book
with profit. Bread and wine will take on a much greater
significance when we apply the lessons spelt out.'
Steve Gaukroger

'This book is a fine combination of theory and practice,
fresh and even innovative. Its value is out of all
proportion to its size.' *John Stott*

ISBN 1 85792 153 4   176 pages

ABOUT THE AUTHOR

Born in Nigeria of missionary parents and converted in his late teens, Rodger Crooks is minister of Belvoir Presbyterian Church, Belfast, Northern Ireland. Previously he worked for twelve and a half years in Dromore, a small town twenty miles south-west of Belfast. Married to Joan for over fifteen years, they have three children – Rosemary, Martyn and Elizabeth. During the 1970s, he read Modern and Ancient History at the Queen's University, Belfast, and studied theology at Union Theological College, Belfast. In 1995, he graduated from Westminster Theological Seminary in Philadelphia with a Doctor of Ministry. As an erstwhile rocker, he enjoys listening to Bob Dylan, Bruce Springsteen, Simon and Garfunkel, and Queen. His other main interest is supporting the greatest soccer team in the world – Manchester United!